The Cop Doc's
Classic Writings on Police Media Relations

Part of

The Cop Doc's Classic Writings
Series of Books

First Edition

Manufactured in the United States of America

ISBN: 978-0-9828697-1-0
(6X9 US trade paperback)

The information contained herein is not to be construed as legal, psychological, or other professional advice. Competent counsel should be sought from the appropriate professional.

www.TheCopDoc.com

The Cop Doc's Classic Writings on Police Media Relations

Part of

The Cop Doc's Classic Writings
Series of Books

By

Police Media Expert & Former Police Chief
Dr. Richard Weinblatt
The Cop Doc

Also by

Dr. Richard Weinblatt

Books

*Reserve Law Enforcement in the United States:
A National Study of State, County, and City Standards
Concerning the Training & Numbers of Non-full-time
Police and Sheriff's Personnel (1993)*

*The Cop Doc's Classic Writings on
Police Careers (2010)*

*Cops & College:
Lessons in Professionalism (2010)*

Also by

Dr. Richard Weinblatt

Columns

. Law and Order:
The Magazine for Police Management
"Reserve Reports"
(1991-2001)

Officer.com
"Reserve Power" and "Career Corner"
(2005-2006)

PoliceLink.com
"Law Enforcement Career Expert"
(2007-Present)

PoliceOne.com
"Weinblatt's Tips" and "Police and the Press"
(2004-Present)

About the Author

Dr. Richard Weinblatt, The Cop Doc, is a law enforcement expert, consultant, writer, radio show host, and media commentator, who has served as a police chief, criminal justice professor, and police academy director. He has worked in several regions of the United States in reserve and full-time sworn positions ranging from auxiliary police lieutenant in New Jersey to Patrol Division Deputy Sheriff in New Mexico to Police Chief in North Carolina.

A certified instructor for Taser, pepper spray, baton, firearms, vehicle operations, and defensive tactics, Dr. Weinblatt instructed and/or oversaw criminal justice degree programs and police academies in Florida, New Mexico, North Carolina, and Ohio.

A well-known police issues commentator for local and national media, Dr. Weinblatt, has been interviewed by the Associated Press, CBS News, CNN, HLN, MSNBC, and The Washington Post among others. He has authored hundreds of articles on law enforcement topics for magazines and websites

Dr. Weinblatt earned a bachelor's degree in Administration of Justice, a Master of Public Administration in Criminal Justice, an Education Specialist degree and a Doctor of Education.

Dr. Weinblatt resides in the greater Orlando, FL, area with his wife, Anne, and son, Michael. Further information is available at www.TheCopDoc.com.

Dedication

This book is dedicated to the men and women whose law enforcement activities make the news and to those who report on policing in their media outlets. As illustrated in the following pages of classic writings, both groups of professionals actually have more commonalities than differences. It is their daily contribution and dedication that affirms our democratic society and its checks and balances.

Acknowledgements

As with any book, many people are involved either directly or indirectly in helping the massive project come to fruition. This book was no different.

The genesis of the material for this particular book in The Cop Doc's Classic Writings series (as well as others in the series) came from the gurus, past and present, of the big law enforcement magazines and websites.

The list of them is long, but mention is certainly warranted of the following individuals that gave the green light to originally publishing these writings: American Police Beat's Cynthia Brown, Corrections Technology & Management's Tim Burke, Law and Order: The Magazine for Police Management's Bruce W. Cameron and Ed Sanow, Officer.com's Tim Dees, Police: The Law Enforcement Magazine's Randall C. Resch and Dennis Hall, PoliceLink.com's Chris Cosgriff and Kevin Powers, and PoliceOne.com's Scott Buhrmaster and Doug Wyllie.

Special attention is accorded to Bruce W. Cameron, the Editor Emeritus of Law and Order: The Magazine for Police Management, as he was the impetus for the writing endeavors back in 1989.

Also of invaluable assistance was the family: Anne, the wifey, and Michael, the munchkin.

Contents

The Cop Doc's
Classic Writings on Media Relations

Introduction

I have carried a badge for many years in different regions of the United States. I've seen some incredible feats of bravery on behalf of my fellow law enforcers. These dedicated public servants put themselves in harm's way for little (and sometimes no) money.

Few things scare these crimefighters. Few that is except for a reporter standing in the lobby waiting for a quick soundbite interview. Armed only with a camera and a microphone, most law enforcement folks I know would rather run down a dark alley, than do an interview with a reporter.

The nation's police departments and sheriff's offices cannot do their mission without the help, cooperation, and information that comes from the public. The main way to do that is through the media: television, radio, and newspapers, as well as increasingly the social media of the Internet (Facebook, Twitter, MySpace, youtube, etc.).

This book on law enforcement media relations draws from almost two decades of my published works. It is part of The Cop Doc's Classic Writings series of books. Those books have been divided by law enforcement topic.

For ease of readership, *The Cop Doc's Classic Writings on Police Media Relations* book has been divided into two parts covering media and community relations. In reality, they are functions that should be intertwined together and integrated into the agency as a whole.

In this book, the writings themselves are a result of my information gathering from some of the best and the brightest folks on the forefront of the law enforcement media and community relations arenas. They also are a reflection of my positive experiences interacting with the media as a law enforcement officer, public information officer (PIO), and police chief. Interestingly, much of my learning in this area has occurred by being a member of the media via my work on police issues as a writer, media commentator for local and national outlets, and radio show host (The Cop Doc radio show: www.blogtalkradio.com/th-cop-doc).

For all of my exposure to the media, I have never felt that I have been unfairly treated. Whether as a law enforcer involved in an investigation or as a "talking head" giving some law enforcement perspective, I have strived to understand what the media is doing and why.

It is my hope that this book will assist others, especially law enforcers and media folks, to understand each other. As is clearly laid out in the third segment of this book, "The image in the mirror: The enemy has a face," the police and the press have more common ground than normally thought.

Dr. Richard Weinblatt
The Cop Doc
Orlando, FL

www.TheCopDoc.com

Police Media Relations

February 1992
Law and Order:
The Magazine for Police Management

The Police and the Media

To Lt. Sadie Darnell, it was just another hot Sunday in August. The 12-year veteran of Gainesville, FL, Police Department was heading to her sister's house for dinner when her on-call beeper signaled an abrupt end to the slow pace.

Darnell's ever-present beeper could hardly have typed out a headline indicative of what was to come. Three years experience as the public information officer was little comfort as she became the center of a media feeding frenzy most police chiefs dread their whole careers.

When five University of Florida students were found brutally murdered, Darnell became the focal point for the media "It was incredible the amount of attention that was paid to this story," she said. She was forced to serve many different constituencies as task force spokesperson.

Many police officials find the prospect of facing such a situation to be anxiety provoking. The title of one police press relations book, "Chief, the Reporters Are Here," infers the inordinate level of fear and distrust law enforcement feels towards the media. The mistrust, often mutual in nature, has done much damage over the years, and has created an unfortunate adversarial relationship.

But what is it that is so dreaded? Why would modern day police officers rather meet a hulking bad guy in a back alley than face a white-collar professional person armed with only a pen and notepad?

Lakewood, CO, Police Lt. Gerald W. Garner, the author of the media relations book mentioned, said the trepidation and distrust comes from a lack of communication and a failure to understand just what each party's responsibilities are. Garner, a 21-year law enforcement veteran who has an undergraduate degree in journalism and a master's in administration of justice, found that many of the police executives attending his media relations class at the FBI National Academy in Quantico, VA, were truly apprehensive of the press.

"By acquainting the police with the press, the 'enemy'; has a face," the former Texas cop and five time book author said.

Interviews with Darnell, Garner and a host of police media experts underscored one clear principle- a working; proactive relationship with the press is an essential component in the success or failure of an agency in its service to the community. Communication is of paramount importance.

A police investigator has to operate in an arena which may range from a lone reporter filling his police blotter column in the local weekly newspaper to a high profile, impromptu news satellite dish city such as the one which sprang up outside of Darnell's office in Gainesville. While the cast of characters may change from jurisdiction to jurisdiction, the concepts remain the similar.

The Internal Conflict

Police officials with an active investigation in progress are very conscious of the dichotomy, which exists in their mandate. On the one hand, cases are solved with information from the public. The police need the press to get to the masses. On the other, police concerns regarding next of kin notification, family suffering and investigation impairment are also bona fide issues and need to be addressed.

"We are only as good as the information we receive," Sheriff Armando B. Fontoura, head of New Jersey's largest sheriff's department based in the city of Newark, said.

"Without public assistance, nothing happens. There has never been a case solved by the FBI without public assistance," Scott A. Nelson, section chief, office of public affairs for the Federal Bureau of Investigation, said. Nelson encouraged law enforcement to be open with the press and recognize the enormous value inherent in the establishment of a two-way dialogue.

San Jose, CA's former police chief, Joseph D. McNamara said, "We need goodwill to be efficient. Without the press, we won't get witnesses. We won't get people dialing 911."

"We view the media as the messenger," Charles Johnston, police chief commanding the 202 officers and agents in Lakewood, CO (a suburb of Denver), said. "We can't reach our residents without them."

McNamara, a frequent guest of high profile journalists such as Ted Koppel and Mike Wallace, said the police need public cooperation in order to do the job. However, he said sometimes the media's requests for information may exceed the department's legal parameters.

Release of Information

The FBI's Nelson said that they have strict disclosure policies, which the 25,000 employees (10,000 special agents) must adhere to. Substantial logistical hurdles must be overcome when you have an investigative organization with that many employees spread out over 56 offices and 17 internationally based legal attaches. However, the U.S. Department of Justice expects all employees to follow the press relations rules set forth in Title 28, Section 50.2 of the Code of Federal Regulations and the Attorney General's Guidelines.

The implication is clear. If it is possible for an organization as far flung as the Federal Bureau of Investigation to successfully formulate clear press policies, there should be no reason for a local criminal justice organization not to be able to do the likewise.

"Clearly, we cannot discuss cases in progress," Nelson said. However, many agencies take this concept too far-thereby involving a total cessation of press communications.

Nelson said that the FBI is sensitive to privacy issues and will not discuss political corruption cases because of the potential damage to reputations. Regarding arrests and indictments in general, Nelson said his employees will release the name, charge and nature of the arrest (whether the individual was armed, etc.). No public identification or discussion of undercover agents, witnesses or law enforcement techniques is allowed.

According to police media expert Dr. Richard R.E. Kania, of the justice and policy studies department at Guilford College in Greensboro, NC, privacy issues must be a major factor in the release decision process. The former Charlottesville, VA, police officer, who has taught media courses at the Southern Police Institute and the University of Louisville, said police administrators should be aware of the immediacy rendered by today's news technology.

We're in the age of the minicams," Kania said. "The demand for news and the ability to physically deliver it often exceeds the propriety of the information being conveyed."

For example, Kania said some next of kin have been informed by radio news reports that a relative has been killed. He said that the notification process in these instances was clearly impaired, as the police were unable to properly apprise them and provide whatever support services might be needed.

Most current police executives recognize the need for confidentiality. The key is for the police executive to develop an adequate level of media sophistication to be able to best determine where the line should be drawn.

"Exceptions come in where the public interest or safety is involved," Nelson said, citing the Sudafed tampering case as a prime example of the public's need to know. Other situations mentioned included civil rights cases and fugitive investigations.

"Once the case is closed and the appeals are done, we will cooperate 100% with all facets of the media," Nelson said.

Det. Lt. Ronald Schmalz, head of the investigation division for the South Brunswick Township, NJ, Police Department agreed and brought up an incentive for the police to interact fully at the appropriate juncture. "After completion of the investigation, I become very open with the press. I use the opportunity to give credit to the detectives and officers involved," Schmalz said.

I definitely view the media as an avenue to show the professional work our people do," Sheriff Fontoura, who once served as a Newark police captain in charge of media relations, said.

Policies Cooperation

Gainesville's Darnell said the crime scene was discovered at 3:30 p.m. and that she was notified at 4:00 p.m. "It would have been a disaster if we had not had policies already in place," she said.

The guidelines should address the aforementioned disclosure issue and more. The policy should be consistent and hold throughout the department, not just the investigative function.

Dr. Ray Surette, professor of criminal justice at Florida International University, said that it is important to develop policies in conjunction with the press. "The media will say 'why should we care about standards if we didn't have anything to do with them.' Do not wait until a critical incident develops to build a relationship," he said.

Responding to the need to educate the media, Lakewood's Chief Johnston asked local print and broadcast reporters to enroll in a citizens' police academy. "They found out what it was like to take a life," Johnston said. "We gave them laser guns and put them through 'shoot, don't shoot' scenarios."

Local police beat reporters delved into a variety of justice issues, which helped, contribute to an understanding of the police service's mission.

Dr. Surette commended Lakewood for implementing the citizens' police academy. He added that he would like to see "the opposite happen- with the police learning more of the media's role, history and function.

"The news media is a business as well as a public information outlet. Law enforcement has to remember the competitive nature of the news business. A chief is asking a lot of a reporter to hold a story," Surette said.

"If you can't talk because of a confidential informant or because of a concern of compromising the investigation, then say so. Don't speak in jargon and don't say 'no comment,'" San Jose's Chief McNamara said.

"Withholding information often results in a worse situation," Dr. Kania agreed."The reporter will probably move on to a second, third, or worse source. Explain honestly why a question cannot be fully answered." He suggests offering other facts that may be useful for the reporter.

Dealing with the press often requires abilities not normally developed within the police structure. "Most chiefs come up through the ranks and are not used to someone questioning their statements. But questioning statements is how reporters make their living," Surette said.

Lt. Darnell found the Gainesville situation attracted reporters with different styles and varying levels of experience. "It was important for us to realize that and respond accordingly," she said.

The Patrol Officer

An important link in the press information process is the street patrol officer. Oftentimes, agencies develop guidelines, which omit the role an officer plays.

Darnell cited the quick actions of Officer Ray Barber as crucial to the integrity of the investigation and the emotional wellbeing of relatives. Barber had received the call to check on the well being of a student and discovered the body- with the parents waiting nearby. "He managed to maintain his composure and control the scene," Darnell said.

"Patrol officers, the first responders, must be schooled on how to handle the situation until the command structure is able to stabilize the area and set up a centralized release process," Det. Lt. Schmalz said.

Other Media Outlets

Beyond the crisis management atmosphere of a sensational crime, police should not lose sight of the media as a vehicle for other messages appropriate for police generated publicity. Of course, such a strategy implies the use of a proactive stance.

Part and parcel of the drive to establish good media relations is a lucid understanding of the different factions of the media. Print, radio, and TV journalists have different needs and obligations.

"TV is visual, newspapers contain data and radio wants quick sound bites. We should cater to their different needs. How to deal with the media is as important as why we should deal with them," Chief Johnston said.

The FBI makes ample use of reality-based television programs such as Fox's "America's Most Wanted." Nelson said police chiefs should satisfy local requests now that there is an interest. The interest may not be there in 10 years.

Nelson said some 3,000 citizen calls are generated from a typical piece on "America's Most Wanted." That program has contributed to the capture of a couple hundred fugitives and approximately 30 million people see the segments that Nelson manages to get on NBC's "Unsolved Mysteries."

In addition to high profile network TV stations, Essex County's Sheriff Fontoura routinely appears with United States Marshal Arthur Borinsky on a local cable show to highlight different fugitives. "We reach more people through TV than we ever could going door to door," he said.

"'Cops,' 'Rescue 911' and the like, show the great work police do. They show the danger on the streets and get sympathy and funding for police functions," Nelson said.

South Brunswick Police Captain Frederick A. Thompson said, "The police haven't learned to market themselves. We will be better cops if the public sees what we do and knows how to assist us in our service to the community."

No longer will a terse "no comment" or a string of police jargon suffice when dealing with the media. On the contrary, appropriate information exchanges with the media, involving public relations and marketing skills, can yield positive results- not all of which would fall under traditional, quantifiable categories.

While the statistics might show a higher clearance rate, not so readily apparent will be the improved morale of the department and heightened awareness on the part of the community. These qualities are ephemeral in nature. It is such combined benefits that will come full circle, impact the statistics, and start to erode the wave of events, which prompt calls for police services.

April 28, 2004
PoliceOne.com

The image in the mirror: The enemy has a face

Law Enforcement personnel are often their own worst enemies when it comes to interacting with the press. This is not due to a lack of intelligence; rather the shortfall comes from a lack of understanding what the media is trying to do. Simple rules can sometimes minimize the confusion. Here are some tips for working effectively with the media:

Reach out

In the mode of proactive community policing, take the initiative and make contact with media representatives in your area. Ask if you can visit the TV and radio station, as well as the newspapers and magazines that cover your jurisdiction. This is an opportunity before anything happens to meet and greet people at many levels of the media organization.

Be Accessible

Much like the modern police administrator, members of the media have bosses and deadlines looming over them. If you are not available before their deadline, they may find someone else with incorrect information to fill up their print or broadcast space. If possible, give them your cell phone number and be sure to answer if they call.

Treat Press Equally

Try not to favor certain members of the media as that will alienate the others. Give the smaller media outlets in your area a lot of your attention. This is especially true if the larger media organizations are not interested in what you are doing. The smaller ones are often more eager and will give your positive version a try as they want to keep your lines of communication open. The larger ones will then follow as they do not want to be left out of the growing story in their area: you.

Have Regular Updates

As with number two above, if a major situation develops, hold regular updates for members of the press so that they can in turn update their audience. Even if you stand in front of the cameras and say that you have no new progress to report, better they hear it from you than someone with less authority or credible information.

No Police Jargon

Stay away from using radio codes or police phrases such as "perpetrator." Use more relaxed and natural phrasing when describing incidents without sounding too casual. Police jargon needs to be clarified for most consumers of the media which uses up precious air time or print space.

Be Brief

Do not be long-winded. The media folks just need the basics of what transpired. The detail required in a police report narrative is not needed by the press.

Avoid Specifics

Be wary of revealing specific information concerning ongoing investigations. As seasoned investigators have learned, some information must be withheld to verify the authenticity of suspects who possess information that only the suspect and the police should know. Information on crime scenes should be vague. Timeline detail should be avoided.

Protect Victims and Witnesses

If you do brief the media on a situation, be sure you make efforts to protect the victim, the victim's family, and any witnesses. All next of kin notifications should be made prior to releasing the names of any deceased individuals. Generally speaking, the presence of witnesses should not be revealed.

Train Media

Encourage inclusiveness by involving the media in positive experiences at your agency. A prime example would be a Citizens Police Academy. The experience will acquaint them with the complexities of modern law enforcement while providing nice exposure for a worthwhile community relations program.

Involve Media

For example, you may set up a media advisory board that reports to the police chief or sheriff. Serving with the agency's public information officer (PIO), these members of different types of press organizations in your jurisdiction will then have a say so on the parameters of the highly important relationship. Issues and grievances can be addressed before they become major distractions. Policy may be set by the agency's chief executive with input from the media. Such involvement will increase the odds that they "buy in" and agree to comply with the policy.

The key to these top ten tips is to open the lines of the communications with the communicators that link us with the citizens we serve. The public does have the right to know. We have the obligation to make sure that any release of information or media access is done in a professional manner that protects our various constituencies.

August 30, 2005
PoliceOne.com

Media relations: Putting a human face on the police

The first "Police and The Press" column for PoliceOne.com covered the concept of putting a face on the image in the mirror. This fourth column goes a step further in calling for that face to be a human one.

Perception is reality

It is helpful to try to look at how the police are perceived by the public. The reality is that most people view the police as stoic individuals who can be almost robotic in their mannerisms and thought processes. As those who have managed officers can attest, law enforcers are among the most passionate and emotional of workers. However, any public display of emotions has been viewed by police executives in the past as unprofessional.

With the advent of 24-hour news channels and Internet news outlets with lots of news material needed, the public has gotten a closer look at policing via the chiefs, sheriffs and spokespersons. Two recent examples have shown how a little emotion honestly displayed actually pulls the public in and helps them make a connection with the police.

Beltway Sniper

In the famous Beltway Sniper case, ten people were killed and three others injured in October 2002. Though many agencies on the federal and local level were involved, the public drew strength from the public presence of then-Montgomery County, Maryland, Police Chief Charles A. Moose. Few could forget his emotional plea to the snipers concerning the danger to children.

The media and the public gravitated to this man who put a face on the largest manhunt in the Washington, D.C., metro area. Chief Moose allowed the public to see that the police truly did care and were doing everything they could to stop the snipers. He became such an ingrained presence to the public that his book and a USA Network made-for-cable TV movie, "DC Sniper: 23 Days of Fear" resulted in much attention and further opportunities to reach out to the community.

Jessica Lunsford

After convicted child molester John Evander Couey confessed in March 2005 to killing 9-year-old Jessica Lunsford, Citrus County, Fla., Sheriff Jeff Dawsey held an emotional live press conference covered by Fox News Channel, CNN and other networks during the Friday night dinner hour.

Sheriff Dawsey didn't take a stance that triggers public frustration with the criminal justice system. Rather than be cold and impersonal in the "just the facts" style of policing, the two-term elected official was obvious in his frustration at not being able to give Jessica back to her family. He was resolute in his belief that he "had the right man."

The steely faced terse "no comment" in police media relations is dead. Modern policing demands public police officials that are able to how that they are in touch with the public while still maintaining a professional demeanor that does not compromise the investigation.

October 19, 2005
PoliceOne.com

The absence of a police marketing mentality

In a February 1992 media relations article I wrote for *Law and Order Magazine*, then captain and now retired police chief Frederick A. Thompson of the South Brunswick Township (NJ) PD lamented the fact that the "police haven't learned to market themselves." The absence of a police marketing mentality was true in 1992, and I think it is still the case in 2005.

While other segments of our society (private corporations, non-profits, etc.) knock on the door of the media in a bid for positive coverage, the police are still reticent to do so. For law enforcement to thrive and serve the community, particularly in the new media world of the Internet, an adoption of the marketing mentality has to take place.

Chief Thompson further related in my 1992 article his belief that, "we will be better cops if the public sees what we do and knows how to assist us in our service to the community." Again, a correct assertion that is even more relevant today.

We are among the most misunderstood of professions. We serve divergent constituencies who have no idea what complexities law enforcers face in a democratic society. I am not advocating that the public be schooled in the intricacies within an agency. Instead, a healthy respect by the community for the professionalism needed to do the job should be developed by the entire LE industry and not just by an isolated agency here and a lone department there.

Marketing mentality example

The medical industry is an example of where years of a unified marketing front in a bid for their survival have made a difference. Doctors make life and death decisions with their service population (although not in the time crunch faced by most patrol officers) much like law enforcement people. Even in this Internet savvy era with people consulting Web MD, there is a historical lack of questioning by their patients. Medical professionals are not nearly as second-guessed as law enforcement folks.

Doctors have changed with the times as they sensed the growing public dissatisfaction with harsh bedside manners. Medical schools now train their residents how to be more customer service oriented and to explain options that are available and why one makes sense over another option. More importantly, the veterans of the industry had to buy into the concept in order for their practices to survive.

Similarly, dentists, who were once the fodder for scary childhood memories, now boast patient selected music and movies during dental exams, along with sedation and patient requested cosmetic dental enhancements.

They have embraced marketing measures aimed at combating their long-held negative public image.

Not only did the industry adopt this horizontally across all organizations, they implemented it vertically, from the top down, within medical practices. Everyone from the doctors to the appointment setters bought in to the marketing mentality. People upset today with the state of health care are less upset with their doctor as they are with their health insurance provider.

The health care field established early on that even though they are there to serve their patients and take an oath, they are also an industry to be marketed. They have some competition and so, as an industry, they were forced to one up each other and, in effect, created an across the board marketing image.

Marketing for officer survival

The police are, in most areas, a monopoly. They do not have competition and few callers for police service have the option to "agency shop." The cop industry has resisted the notion that they all must change to survive. The prevailing thought has been: There's crime, so there's job security.

Officer survival instructors call that complacency, and it is not a healthy mindset. The crime/job security approach is a flawed way of thinking as evidenced by the layoffs of officers in many cities across the nation. Michigan, Ohio and Pennsylvania are examples of states where the police recently lost jobs and were not viewed by the public as THE budgetary priority.

If the public, and in turn their elected representatives running the political machinery that makes the staffing decisions, truly were targeted with the adoption of a nation-wide police marketing mentality, then layoffs and budget cuts would be curtailed. The politicians would know that the police budget was a sacred cow not to be slashed.

Much like those bandied about regarding community policing, proactive measures have to be taken in order for the cop marketing machine to have an impact. The reactive mold of public information has to be broken and recast. We need horizontal and vertical integration within all agencies of this new marketing approach that involves each member of the department.

We need to step forward and take advantage of the inordinate interest that the public has in police matters. Just look at the lineup of primetime TV shows and best-selling books. For years the fictional police have been the centerpiece and have captivated the public's attention. The same holds true for the Internet's websites and blogs, as well as television news.

Proactive news appearances

Doctors have become a staple of morning news shows extolling the virtues of everything from cardiac health to plastic surgery.

Question: how many police chiefs and public information officers do you see on a regular basis that appear on local and national TV news programs? How many even know how to convey their message in a natural and camera friendly manner? Answer: perhaps a handful. The majority of the time you see a PIO it is in response to a criminal investigation.

The police have a built in advantage in our society that lends itself to the success of a marketing mentality. Not even the medical profession can lay claim to such an opportunity. Not every newspaper has a medical correspondent, but they all have police reporters.

With a police marketing mentality, the positive stories on policing and those hardworking men and women who serve should vastly outnumber the crime driven and negative, department scandal driven items. We would finally keep pace with and perhaps surpass the fictionalized version of policing embedded in society's psyche. Only then would the true nature of law enforcement's service to the community be known and believed by the public.

January 16, 2006
PoliceOne.com

Press releases: Used and abused

Here is a very common question that I get from police chief and public information officer (PIO) types: "What is the appropriate use of press releases in police media relations?" Back in the '80s, when I owned a New York City metro public relations firm, the uses of press releases were the staple of the much smaller media industry. But the rules have changed since then. This Police and the Press column covers how and when you should use press releases so that you do not use and abuse them or, for that matter, your media contacts.

Press releases have long been an area of confusion and even the right name is an elusive prey. Some prefer the traditional moniker of "press release," whereas I gravitate more to the use of the term "news release." The word "news" connotes information that is credible and worthy of a reader's (and hence the reporter's or assignment desk's) attention. "Press release" sounds like a puff piece generated by a publicity flack.

News releases can run the gamut from soft feature items, such as a police volunteer of the month recognition program, to hard news stories, such as the release of the name of the deceased in a motor vehicle collision. The two types of releases feed off of each other and solidify your dealings with the media. That is especially helpful when a departmental crisis erupts and your established, positive relationship with the press can stave off negative publicity.

Identify message and target

Before even crafting your news release, you will need to identify what you want to say and then figure out who is your target audience. What is the message that you are trying to impart and who should get that message? Connecting with Internet captivated teenagers is different from elderly folks who tend to be larger readers of local, weekly hometown newspapers.

Researching your dissemination targets and appropriate distribution points to get the message out is key. You need to figure out whom you want to reach and how to communicate your message.

More traditional releases are appropriate when trying to reach a more mature audience that has long established channels of information gathering. Younger people have non-traditional sources for their information, such as the Internet. News releases for the Internet tend to be shorter reflecting on-screen reading habits and shortened attention spans.

Newspapers

One key media outlet that has been mentioned, hometown weekly newspapers, has long been a target rich environment for older town residents. They are very interested in what their neighbors and their law enforcement agency are up to.

Weekly papers and their brethren are ideal for static stories that are not likely to change and do not have a pressing time deadlines. A story on an upcoming Citizens Police Academy or the release of a department's annual report are but two of many examples that could fit into this format.

These venues look for releases that are complete and can function as stand-alone articles. Short-staffed, budget-strapped, and over-worked, weekly papers love to print these releases in their entirety. It is important to adhere to good journalistic principles, as well as to copy the writing style of your target paper. Customization is important, as one size does not fit all publications. And don't forget smaller monthly or alternative format publications in your area.

Daily newspapers are larger operations that tend to do more of their published material with in-house staff reporters. Your releases for these media folks should be a little shorter than that employed for the weekly and monthly outlets. The news release should give them just enough information so that they will want to create a feature story highlighting your agency's news or initiative.

The news release will need to be clear why the information is newsworthy and also why it should be covered now. DUI prevention and enforcement around New Year's Eve is an example of a story where timing is key.

Radio

Local radio stations are also a good place to contact to get your message out. Even with low wattage, local radio hosts engender a fiercely loyal following. They function in short sound bites so short news releases are more appropriate for them, although producing an audio news release for them is another option.

Internet radio is a new and often overlooked medium. Many people in your city most likely have launched their own radio stations given the economic feasibility of the Internet. The audience tends to be larger, and certainly younger, than you might think.

The short news release is probably the better route as it may lead to an invitation into the radio station's studios. If you handle it correctly, you may be able to springboard into longer format live interviews with listener phone call segments.

Television

Broadcast television stations that cover your area are but another distribution points for your news release. In the TV venue, you are again looking to produce short, sound-bite quality nuggets of information. Public service announcements (PSAs) are classic examples.

Local cable TV systems often have a public access channel with programming geared to local matters. You should watch these sometimes roughly produced local talk shows to see if you fit in as a guest to tout the topic of your release. The hosts may be a bit eccentric, but a little preparation will help you to manage the interview. Showcasing your agency's new K-9 team is a good visual image that works well in a TV studio.

Local text information cable TV channels should also be targets of your customized releases. They need a steady diet of information to put on the screen, but the information should be put in a bullet point format or other style that they use. You want to make it easy for them to load the information into the chyron and put on the screen. Date and time specific events, such as National Night Out, work well in this outlet.

If you want to reach younger people, do not overlook campus based high school and college newspapers. Make sure that their targeted news release features something that would be of interest to their readers. Two examples might be a new Corvette marked police car recently confiscated from a drug dealer and a police initiative to enforce underage and prom night drinking issues.

The danger of working with young reporters is their lack of experience and tendency to interject their own preconceived notions into the article. A detailed news release that leaves little room for conjecture, along with your personal contact with the adult faculty newspaper advisor, should alleviate that problem.

News release distribution

Once you have identified your target market media distribution points and crafted your customized news release, you will need to decide how to actually get the material to them. It used to be that all releases went via "snail mail." Nowadays, some reporters only deal in email. On the flip side, other reporters have found their inboxes clogged with releases and end up deleting or routing them to bulk mail folders. Still others like FAXs. You will need to make a few contacts to see how each target outlet wants to receive their information.

After the releases are sent out, a follow-up system should come into play. Press folks, especially those at larger media outlets, get inundated with releases of different types. You have a built in advantage as a representative of the local police or sheriff's department. You are engaged in public service and everyone is interested in the police. Just look at the huge prime-time TV line up of crime shows.

Time when to call the media representative for your release follow-up. Deadlines are a major issue for these people. Generally speaking, newspapers are best called before lunch and far away from afternoon article deadlines. Radio people need to be called during that small window when they get off the air. TV folks tend to be more receptive when you reach them in the early afternoon before they get ready for their evening news broadcasts.

Don't start off by asking them if they got the release. The better approach involves asking them if they need any other information. It's a polite way to remind them of the release that they may have only glanced out earlier, but has some good story potential for them. Make written notes for requests to contact them again the next day and the like.

Press conferences

News releases are handy as supplements to a formal press conference or field-based press briefing. Solid information, such as the spelling of a suspect's name or a lost child's full description, can be given out with the chance of reporting error minimized. The hard copy new release you hand out eliminates the need for the reporter to quickly scribble down information that may be read erroneously later at his or her newsroom computer terminal.

Reporters, especially those television journalists looking for visual images, will appreciate you standing up and talking to them, while still providing the news release that gives them an easy and convenient way of getting the nitty-gritty information.

Most media types will be responsive to you. As stated previously, you represent local law enforcement and are an important source of the press' bread and butter: news. They need you as much as you need them. A good, customized and targeted news release can be the genesis of a positive relationship.

April 20, 2007
PoliceOne.com

Tips for major incident media relations in the wake of the Virginia Tech shooting

In the wake of the horrific Virginia Tech shooting, the important role of the media, especially the *New* Media, has become especially clear. Many of the students in the shooting incident lamented a lack of information and, interestingly, that much of their information came from the Internet.

Major incidents, such as that which transpired in Blacksburg, VA, are vehicles of confusion. Today's situation should illustrate to even the haters of media that the press served a vital role in getting the word out. Virginia Tech's campus police could in no way do that by themselves. A great, previously established relationship and a proactive stance is the way to go.

So, given that great relationship, what needs to happen when "the big one" hits your jurisdiction? Here's a review:

1. Set up a perimeter and place your command post and press briefing areas (they should be separate) well out of the active scene. In the case of bombings, such as what happened in Georgia, secondary devices can be rigged to go off to injure responding officers and deputy sheriffs, as well as officials at the command post.

2. Have regular briefings by an established public information officer (PIO) or law enforcement executive. In the case of multi-agency involvement, one person should become the face of the law enforcement effort. Former Montgomery County (MD) Police Chief Charles Moose was a prime example of this during the beltway sniper situation.

3. Avoid the clichés of "no comment." Media folks will go elsewhere to produce the story if you don't give them some information. That elsewhere may be sources that have misinformation or even a contrary agenda.

4. Be aware of your state and local laws and policies regarding open records and "sunshine" concepts. You may be limited in what you can withhold from the media.

5. With number four in mind, take care not to give so much information that impair the ongoing enforcement and rescue efforts or the impending investigation. Names of involved persons should be redacted from statements pending notification of next of kin.

6. Any specific information that is released should be done in written press release form to avoid mistakes when the media reproduces the material. Better yet, the information should also be sent out in electronic form (emails) and posted to the press release section of the agency's website.

7. Use other websites as well. In the case of a campus shooting, the college website should be used. In a longer, drawn out information campaign, student blogs can be a powerful ally and give the agency a voice to an audience they have trouble normally reaching.

The new media is a key component in the modern police chief or sheriff's bid to reach out. We see that clearly and most recently in the Virginia Tech shooting. Many students have already reported that they got their information from the Internet. News websites and blogs have become the town center where news and ideas are exchanged. Police and sheriff's departments need to be on the cutting edge of this media movement in order to get the word out and better serve a rapidly evolving society.

August 22, 2008
PoliceOne.com

What law enforcement can learn from the Caylee Anthony case

You would have to be under a rock not to notice the large volume of press coverage garnered by the Caylee Anthony missing child case here in Orlando, FL. Police professionals interested in how the media interacts with law enforcement should take special notice of the media's quest for information in the Caylee Anthony case.

As someone with law enforcement and media interviewing experience, who lives and works in the area, it's not terribly surprising to be asked by local press to grant interviews on the topic – many of which are on PoliceOne's sister site, BLUTube. Even more than before, this investigation has lead to an incredible number of people coming up to me seeking answers to their many questions.

To their credit, the Orlando-based Orange County Sheriff's Office has handled the media onslaught quite well. They have offered some information, but have kept quiet when such information might impair the integrity of their investigation. As I have said many times, including when I was a police chief and had to contend with the media following a homicide or other high profile crimes, if law enforcement agencies and experts ("commentators" in media parlance – a group in which I now find myself) do not interact with the media, other, less responsible parties will step in and fill the void.

Those other folks, while colorful and entertaining (and useful in boosting TV ratings) frequently work at odds with law enforcement and spew out misinformation. The Caylee Anthony case proves once again that it is incumbent upon us as professionals in the field to fill up that airtime with responsible information.

We can't censor the press nor should we be able to do so in a democratic society. We can't stop them from using as talking heads any person they deem appropriate. But what we can do is provide them with meaningful statements grounded in solid law enforcement training, educational credentials, and experience. And we can do so in an open and non-defensive manner.

All too often, law enforcement agencies circle the wagons when they see the media approaching and issue a terse "no comment." That way of doing business has long gone the way of the covered wagon. Ask yourself: "Has my agency gotten savvy in its dealings with the media?"

If they haven't become progressive in their approach, than they need to do so.

The media here in Central Florida, as well as nationally (think CNN Headline News' "Nancy Grace" or Fox News Channel's "On The Record with Greta Van Susteren"), has been hungry for any perspective. News executives have told me in their offices that their "numbers are up" (that means ratings) and that the "Caylee story has worked for them."

To that end, the media folks have consulted psychics such as The Body Hunters. Doesn't it make more sense for them to talk with trained professionals with proven track-records? I like to think that my commentary filled up some airtime and prevented even more fringe folks from confusing viewers.

And now we have the emergence of the bail bonds man from Sacramento, CA, Leonard Padilla, as well as PR handler Larry Garrison of Natalie Holloway and John Mark Karr fame. At the same time, the airtime is being filled up with more noteworthy events such as Hurricane Fay. The hurricane further illustrates my point that the media must burn minutes to make its money.

It's been a long time since I wrote my first law enforcement media related article in February 1992. Now that we are in the era of the 24-hour news cycle with its insatiable appetite, the need to interact with the media is underscored now more than it ever was in that old article. Dated, but not out-dated, the concepts I felt were true then are even more true today.

Police chiefs, sheriffs, public information officers, and other interested parties should take heed of the lessons of the Caylee Anthony media storm. I believe that we will see more and more of these types of cases played out very publicly with armchair sleuths scrutinizing what their tax dollar-supported law enforcers are doing to solve the mystery.

August 2008
PoliceLink.com

Professionalism and PoliceLink: What does your badge stand for?

With all of the recent buzz on PoliceLink.com concerning how people should conduct themselves on the website, I thought I'd weigh in with a reminder of who we are and what our badges stand for: professional law enforcement officers who are bound by a higher moral and ethical code of conduct.

All of us, rookies and veterans alike, need to remind ourselves of why we are involved in the law enforcement field. I hope your answer has as a component to help people. We are not supposed to be bullies. When we talk about law enforcers, my six-year-old son, Michael, put it in simple terms: "police officers help people, Daddy. They are not mean or hurt people's feelings." From the mouths of babes comes the wisdom that we should draw from. I, for one, concur with my very wise little boy.

I have long been appalled by the lack of an adherence to professional conduct by what is a vocal minority. As PoliceLink guru Chris Cosgriff pointed out in his forum post, hundreds of other members have been upset at the meanness. Many members, such as me, my wife, Anne, and numerous others I have heard from avoid the forums because of their propensity to turn mean at the hands of a relative few.

It is not a professional law enforcement officer's role to be judge and jury and "come down" on members who, for example, make the "fatal" mistake of misspelling "Special" in their "Special Agent" title description in their profile. It is not professional to bully and pick on a 16-year-old boy who wants to be a police officer and in his zeal says a few wrong things. Haven't we all made some mistakes when we were 16? And it certainly is not professional to taunt and say that Chris Cosgriff, who founded an honorable site like ODMP and toils on PoliceLink late into the night, has lost a piece of his anatomy. I was embarrassed beyond belief for my profession to see those kind of statements in the forums.

We, as defenders of the weak in society, should not be bullies. We should not be power hungry. Rather, we should empower people to reach their potential in their own lives and the lives in their community. If someone says something or spells something wrong, denigration should not be the path for us as professionals. Rather, education and compassion should be our mantra. In a nutshell, we need to take the high road and not be baited into, whether intentionally or unintentionally, a vitriolic back and forth.

Us versus Them

This is not an "us versus them" profession anymore. The days of circling the wagons to defend outrageous statements or conduct by a LEO just because they have a badge are over. Circling the wagons went out with the covered wagons.

I understand where this mentality comes from. I worked in a busy, call-to-call type of jurisdiction. In that context, it's easy to view all civilians as bad as we see the few at their worst and they come to represent all non-law enforcement folks. I understand how the cynicism can creep in. But it is our job as professionals to resist that dark view of society.

This business of people having little standing or basis to form a respectfully phrased opinion unless they are have graduated from a police academy and are verified law enforcement is just not becoming for our profession. I have made many presentations, publicly, as well as in academic settings, where people disagreed, for example, with my backing of the availability of the Taser for officers in appropriate use of force situations.

My response was not to cut them down with "what do you know? You're not, nor have you ever been, a LEO, so you don't know anything." Rather, I used the opportunity to educate and inform in a respectful manner. Sometimes I got my message across. Sometimes I did not.

What I did get almost all of the time was an acknowledgment that I did not act condescending and respected their opinion. The person may have not agreed with me, but at least we had a level of mutual respect that was not stopped just because I represent the criminal justice field. Respectful discourse...that's what we do in the United States of America.

Professional Conduct

We are not a dictatorship in this country. That is why sheriffs and police chiefs (whether directly or indirectly) report to the civilian electorate. When the police think they know it all and as a result can control civilian enterprises, such as PoliceLink, it is dangerous to our profession. Disagreements and unprofessional conduct should be taken to private venues such as PM or other venues.

I believe, and indeed applaud, PoliceLink's recent and long awaited movement to demand a professional level of conduct is good. PoliceLink is not "owned" or "controlled" by the police. We do not have the legal or moral authority to hijack a private website that would not be here if it were not for the initial risk of capital and the ongoing sweat equity put forth by Affinity Labs' Chris Michel, PoliceLink's Chris Cosgriff and their colleagues. It is Affinity's call to action, and now Monster's duty too, to police their own private enterprise.

While I am all for freedom of speech, it has to be done in a responsible manner. Our society is bound by certain rules of conduct. For example, you don't yell "fire" in a crowded theater. Private establishments can expect an even higher standard of conduct as long as its rules are not used as a basis to discriminate against certain people (for example people of color or women).

Affinity Labs and Monster have the right to demand higher codes of conduct in the discussion forums. Just like in clubs and restaurants across this great country, as long as it is not done in a discriminatory basis, management has the right to refuse service to anyone that does not conduct him or herself in accordance with management's interpretation of the rules. Period. That is their right and, as a founding member of PoliceLink, long-time writer, and law enforcement professional, I defend it.

Off-Duty Conduct

Even worse yet, are the members of the general public who step into the public sections of this site and are appalled at the unprofessional comments in forums (and on the videos as well). Those nasty comments cement in their minds their preconceived stereotypes of officers as power mad and mean-spirited. And cops sometimes wonder why so many people hate a badge bearer...that's why.

Of course, as representative of law enforcement, we have an even higher standard than that exacted by private establishments. Most agencies in our country rightfully regulate the behavior of on AND off-duty officers and expect that they do not discredit their badge or agency. It's because the public sees our actions and negative conduct damages the efforts of all hard-working men and women who strive for excellence in dispensing law enforcement services every day.

As expected, agencies are scrutinizing officers' online behavior, postings, pictures, etc. and I warn our police academy students here when they start their 770 hour academy-based transformation to clean up their Internet profiles and web presence. From DUIs and domestic incidents to online bullying and posting naked pictures on the web, officers and deputy sheriffs are fired for conduct unbecoming their chosen profession in words and deeds, in their communities and on the Internet. Anytime we are in public, we are scrutinized by the public. That is a fact of life and the PoliceLink forums are no exception.

It is not the conduct that most readers would want their mother, father, brother, sister, husband, wife, boyfriend, or girlfriend to see or read. What separates us from the predators and bullies of society is not our badge. It is what our badge stands for in terms of the conduct and behavior we display. So I ask you, as I join PoliceLink in demanding a higher standard of conduct from our law enforcement professionals using the website, what does your badge stand for?

August 3, 2009
PoliceOne.com

There's a new Sheriff in this media town

With the tragedy of Byrd and Melanie Billings, the adoptive parents murdered near Pensacola, Florida, recently, Escambia County top lawman David Morgan has become the face of the investigation and has embraced many of the most effective concepts for the conduct of media relations by law enforcement. The first-term Sheriff has been a fixture on national shows, filling the void in the 24-hour news cycle that would otherwise be filled by those with other agendas.

As I wrote in my first article about the conduct of media relations (back in 1992), and have repeated many times here on PoliceOne, it is incumbent upon us as law enforcement professionals to embrace the media in a democratic society. We need to reach out and bridge barriers that exist between the general public and us.

As the first upswing in officer deaths in years is being tallied, we are reminded that the best officer safety is not that fancy new gun or house clearing technique (although those are nice). Rather, it is to create an atmosphere of respect. Most people (albeit not everyone) who come to view law enforcers as fellow stakeholders in the community with a human touch will in turn help to protect and foster cooperation. A respectful tone, in person and in the media, is the key to this equation.

Professional Demeanor

Sheriff Morgan, a long-time military member who retired at the rank of major, has perfected that respectful and professional on-air tone with his "yes, sir" and "yes, ma'am" phrases. He's consistent with that approach as he makes the rounds from the CBS Early Show to Anderson Cooper's AC360 on CNN. To his credit the sheriff understands the sophisticated approach he needs to take with the media. As he told the Associated Press in an interview, Escambia County "isn't Mayberry anymore."

Nor is the field of law enforcement. Gone is the bad stereotype of the cigar-chomping flatfoot speaking of perpetrators and using incomplete sentences heavily laden with incomprehensible police jargon. His terms are ones that the public can relate to, such as "humdinger." You have to love it. This man speaks plainly, but respectfully. The media and the public like that in a law enforcer.

The Sheriff has very astutely given the investigation, and consequently law enforcement, a human face. Contrary to what many folks think, we in blue (and green, brown, etc.) do care. The cameras were there when Sheriff Morgan interacted with representatives of the family. They recorded the resolve that the Sheriff and his deputies had in cracking the case.

Investigative Integrity

Of course, the usual lament from veteran investigators is that media involvement will impair the integrity of the investigation. I heard it when as a police chief I alerted the media following a homicide. Credit goes to Sheriff Morgan for acknowledging that when discussing the aspect of the safe that was recovered at one of the suspect's properties. He clearly understands the balancing act between the public's "right to know" and our need for tips from the community versus the need to withhold certain key pieces of information. He understands that one of those big reasons is to help ascertain the veracity of statements that self-described suspects may come up with.

At no time does one get the feeling watching this justice executive walk the media tight rope. Anyone who has been on the other end of the questioning microphone can attest that the media is good at trying to get information. Sheriff Morgan never lost his cool. He was able to answer the questions along the lines of his talking points and would not be bullied to stray off the path.

The Sheriff, like law enforcement folks should, obviously noted the 24-hour news cycle and appeared not sleep. He seemed to know that if he did not provide the talking head commentary, someone else would be sought out by the booking producers. That person or persons may hurt the investigation and the image of the Escambia County Sheriff's Office. The Sheriff knew he had to be available when the media needed him and fulfilled that part of his post quite well.

All criminal justice folks, especially those in executive posts empowered to speak with the media, should view themselves as ambassadors for their agency and policing. We need to reach out and encourage interaction with the community. We need to, as Sheriff Morgan has, put a human face on law enforcement.

August 25, 2009
PoliceOne.com

Top 10 social networking tips for cops

In the wake of the widely known Texas waitress photos which led to the firing of one Midland County deputy sheriff and the suspension of three others, a look at how online technology has impacted the world of the law enforcement officer seemed to be warranted. This is not a new occurrence. Recall if you will the Hoboken, NJ, SWAT team disbanded following "racy" Hooters girl pictures bearing weaponry on police vehicles. The self-replicating Internet made sure that everyone eventually saw the pictures in question.

As someone who oversees Basic Police Academies, currently in Ohio and previously in Florida, I have long advised students on the benefits of the wise use of an online persona. While some officers totally bypass any use of online sites in a bid to protect themselves in the future, I view that as throwing the baby out with the bath water. I advocate a more controlled use of those outlets.

I personally make much use of technology having accounts on a variety of websites including Facebook, Twitter, MySpace, youtube, Blogger, and Linkedin among others. I have for many years, including when I served as a police chief, with no negative consequences.

These are useful tools for personal and professional networking and communication. I use the analogy that any tool, including firearm and Taser, can be abused. It is the professional officer that knows how to use these technology tools responsibly and in accordance with departmental policies and community morals.

Many officers have forfeited an otherwise promising career for a few moments of posting euphoria. While other folks may garner only a chuckle in response to their online adventures, a professional law enforcer is held to a higher standard by most employing agencies.

The phenomenal growth of technological innovation has impacted law enforcement from the advent of digital photography to the omnipresent social network Facebook. This article offers tips for using the new online technologies while not sacrificing your career.

1) No gun glorification. While this may upset the Second Amendment supporters out there, the reality is that many of the public does not like to see a glorification of firearms in pictures of law enforcers.

Quite a few officers have lost their jobs after posing with weaponry in a way perceived as offensive or too warrior oriented.

While the depiction of guns in the course of their normal scope and use is not problematic, aiming the gun at the camera seems to be the trigger for the pink slip. Shots of officers engaged in their normal course of fire at the gun range have not appeared to bring about a backlash. Posing with weaponry, involving either the officer or (worse yet) a civilian, has historically been problematic for the employee.

2) No alcohol. Officers have also found themselves in the hot seat after posting pictures of them partying and drinking alcohol. Many agencies view this to be contrary to a professional image. Of even more concern is that sometimes others identified in the pictures turn out to be minors in possession of alcohol which itself opens up another can of issues.

3) Watch your comments. This is an important one. Posted comments on social networking sites are being dragged into legal proceedings especially when use of force is involved. Comments that imply the officer enjoys using force on people, especially certain groups of people, are being seized on by criminal defense and civil plaintiffs' attorney to show the officer had a pre disposition to be physical or has a documented bias against their client.

Be mindful that discussion boards and the like are a public written record of your communication. Like reports and radio dispatch conversations, they can be discovered and frame your actions in a context that you may not like. Much like reports, if you don't want it dragged into the legal arena, don't type it online.

4) Avoid department bashing. Another area that has gotten some officers into hot water, the First Amendment freedom of speech notwithstanding, are comments that bash the agency. Depending on how it is framed, it could open you up to administrative charges and possibly civil liability. More and more bloggers and online posters are being held responsible for their critical speech online. Especially if it is later proved that the postings lack a factual basis and are intended to damage the target of the criticism.

At the very least, launching such a site or contributing to an existing website that bashes the agency does not endear you to the powers that be or position you as a team player ripe for promotion.

5) Restrict personal information. Much like we can use Facebook and the like as a tool to find people and research information, so too can the bad guys. Be judicious in the posting of information and pictures. For example, some officers will not use pictures of their family members or going even further, of themselves. Others, like me, withhold their cell phone number.

6) Picture Choice. Make sure that the pictures that you do choose to post don't have any of the aforementioned problem areas or have nudity. Many officers, including myself, have shirtless bodybuilding or fitness oriented photos online. That is not a problem. The topless woman drinking at the party with you exemplifies what is a problem.

7) Minimize status update complaints. In this era of economic contraction, there are many people waiting in line for your spot in the agency. Administrators know this. We've all seen the officers that post their status with complaints about the shift, their sergeant, or the job. I've heard some supervisors who state, after reading such negatively tinged status updates, let so and so "find another job if they are so unhappy here."

While not every job is going to be great each and every day, gripes should not be aired via status updates. The agency may only be too happy to find someone else that would appreciate them.

8) Highlight accomplishments. Many look to Facebook, Linkedin, and the like as electronic resumes. Take advantage of that and use it to highlight your professional accomplishments. Post pictures of you learning some new technique (being careful not to show scores or other information). Post status updates of that advanced training course you take.

9) Set privacy settings. While I have my online presence open to the public, many have privacy settings

that restrict access to family and friends that you have predetermined. While not foolproof, the settings should keep most interlopers locked out of your pages.

10) When in doubt, leave it out. I have long coached academy students and officers to pretend that I am perched on their shoulder and watching what they are doing. In the same vein, they could have their mother hovering overhead. If you wouldn't want us to see it or if either of us would be displeased with what is being contemplated to go online, it probably is not a good idea to upload it.

Police Community Relations

Summer 1993
21st Century Policing:
The New Jersey Community Policing Newsletter

Volunteer Officers and Community Policing

In the spirit of police executives across New Jersey and the Nation, Mount Holly Police Chief James F. Hansen explained how his 2.9 square mile Burlington County municipality was divided into eleven sectors in order to address quality of life concerns. The importance of joining the police and the community as a team to tackle problems has been clearly established.

What stands out about Chief Hansen's aggressive approach to the concept is that Class II. Special Law Enforcement Officer David Perez, a resident of Mount Holly, has responsibility for sectors also. "David is bilingual and it is beneficial for us to have such an officer who lives in a part of town where there are a lot of Spanish speaking people," said Hansen who added that Perez' duties also involve freeing up full-time officers for more pressing matters.

Hansen is not alone in the Garden State in utilizing auxiliary or special police officers to help bridge the gap between the police and community.

Considered to be the ultimate in community policing, this approach brings the community into the police and police into the community.

Police officers tend to associate with other police officers, whereas the reserve component of the department has ties to both the civilian and police segments. The auxiliary or special officer becomes the conduit through which each side gains and understanding of the positions of all involved.

Auxiliaries and specials have full-time jobs and assist their full-time counterparts on a part-time or volunteer basis. They receive their training and serve their agencies during hours which do not conflict with their full-time, day occupations.

In accordance with the Special Law Enforcement Officers (SLEO) Act of 1986, New Jersey special police officers are certified by the New Jersey Police Training Commission (PTC), the same body that regulates full-time officers. And they must complete their training prior to being deployed in the field. Special officers may or may not be paid at the discretion of the employing entity and are certified by a PTC approved academy at one of two levels.

Class I. officers receive an average of 78 hours of training. They enforce municipal ordinance, Title 39 motor vehicle laws, and non-indictable offenses. They are unarmed, but may carry handcuffs, side-handle batons, etc.

Class II. special officers have full police powers and are armed while on duty. They undergo an average of 452 hours of training. Many academies exceed the 452 hours. The Gloucester County Police Academy in Deptford conducts a grueling 625 hours Class II. academy.

Auxiliary officers in the Garden State are under the regulation of the New Jersey State Police Office of Emergency Management and may not be paid. They must receive a minimum of 42 hours of pre-service training, although many academies far exceed that number. Essex County's auxiliaries get 77 hours of training in Cedar Grove and Middlesex County's Edison-based auxiliary academy comes in at 88. Their service must be oriented to training objectives and they cannot replace full-time officers.

Auxiliary police officers have full police powers while on duty and may be armed at the discretion of the Chief of Police upon completion of a PTC firearms course. Essex County's Bloomfield, Essex Fells, Irvington, Maplewood, Roseland, and South Orange have armed volunteer auxiliaries. The Passaic County Police Academy in Wayne Township, NJ, runs an 80 hours firearms course for auxiliary officers.

In Perth Amboy, Detective William "Willie" Lopez, the auxiliary police liaison officer who oversees the 118-memner department's community relations efforts has put his auxiliary officers on bicycles on the waterfront and other key areas of the 52,000 population Middlesex County city. The 15 year veteran, who spent two years as a Los Angeles police officer in South Central L.A., said the 33 volunteer auxiliary officers are the ambassadors of the city and help to reverse the negative image the community has of the police.

"We deal with people on a human level and break the macho cop stereotype that people have of cops," said Alvin Gauthier, an auxiliary sergeant with seven years of service.

Perth Amboy auxiliaries have a directed patrol plan which includes the railroad station and downtown areas. Detectives have used the officer as an interpreter in investigations including a rape case.

Auxiliary and special officers are often put in the field to tackle a particular type or geographical area problem. In Camden County, Hadden Township Class I. specials have been instrumental in curtailing underage drinking.

In the City of Long Branch, NJ, Captain Patrick Caron, Director of Public Safety, has used Class II. special officers on the boardwalk and during large events such as parades. The specials that get 415 hours of training over the course of nine months at the Monmouth County Police Academy have done well. He plans to use volunteer officers in the downtown section of the city to assist with foot patrols.

In addition to their basic training, the volunteer/part-time officers often go at their own expense to in-service training courses. It is part of the movement among reservists themselves to upgrade and professionalize. In great part due to the litigious environment that police administrators operate in the old civil defense mentality is falling by the wayside as a higher standard and level of expectation is being applied to the officers.

Among the auxiliaries who have become Monadnock PR-24 certified instructors are Cranford's Brian M. Lopez, Eatontown's Thomas Gross, Perth Amboy's Michael A. Chrone and Bloomfield auxiliary sergeant William Vloyanetes who is a Doppler Radar operator and a certified firearms and PR-24 instructor.

New Jersey's auxiliary and special officers like the quarter of a million reservists who serve across the nation have become an integral part of the law enforcement landscape.

April 1997
Law and Order:
The Magazine for Police Management

Bicycles: More Than Just a Balancing Act

According to Seattle Police Department Sgt. Paul D. Grady (arguably the father of modern law enforcement bicycle patrols), police biking has rolled much farther than the mere science of balancing on two wheels. Driven by the citizenry's call for more pedal police and proponents such as Grady, officers on bicycles are here to stay.

"Our administration is very much supportive. It's also the number one thing residents tell us they want to see," said Sgt. Mary Schofield, a supervisor in the Las Vegas Metropolitan Police Department's bike patrol.

The Las Vegas bike unit is busting the myth that bicycle officers are not engaged in proactive law enforcement beyond their public relations guise. "Each of our two-bike teams makes four to six arrests a night," Shofield said.

"It's common for us in Seattle to swoop down and literally grab the drugs out of a dealer's hands," Grady said. He emphasizes the vital role the pedal pushers have in battling the drug pushers.

Garnering accessibility with the requisite speed needed to respond to the rigors of the job, law enforcement officers on police mountain bikes have found homes in diverse settings such as the NYPD patrolled housing projects of New York City, the frozen fairways of Canada, and the parks, malls, and downtowns of main street America.

The advantages cited are numerous and well-known. Bicycles provide mobility to go where vehicles can't, costs less than vehicles, silent, tactical approaches possible, and enhances community relations and interaction.

As with most "hot" concepts that rocket to public view, misconceptions abound concerning the law enforcement bike brigades. "One of the biggest misconceptions is that it's a glamorous job. But it's not just a P.R. unit," said Sgt. Kevin DeVillenfagne of the City of Calgary Police in Canada. He pointed out that their constables often take their bikes and prisoners onto the transit system for the trip to booking.

"The element of surprise is how we get them," beamed a proud Grady. He said that the Seattle Police downtown squad is very proactive in its approach. The bike officers make around five times the number of drug arrests on foot patrol. The agency has some 100 officers on bikes.

Las Vegas has a streamlined booking system which enables their bike officers to make four to six arrests per night. A transportation van provides prisoner transport.

"We like the bikes because the officers can come out of wooded paths in our housing developments and surprise residential burglars with their speed and silence," said South Brunswick Township, NJ, Police Captain and FBI National Academy graduate Frederick A. Thompson.

Police bikers don't always come out on top, however, and the assignment has it dangers. All those interviewed emphasized the importance of team riding. An Inkster, MI, police officer on a bike was killed in 1994 while working alone.

"Since the bike goes where the car can't, how is the car going to provide back-up?" Grady asked. "Bike officers should ride in pairs, especially in urban areas."

Grady, a 16-year police veteran who pioneered the bike patrol concept in Seattle in 1987 is a passionate advocate for bike training. "A large problem we have is a failure to adequately train our bike officers. While the use of bikes has caught on, not all realize the importance of a good training program," he said.

Grady, who serves as executive director of the Law Enforcement Bicycle Association, also teaches a four day (32 hour) Police Mountain Bike Training Course, as well as a 40-hour version. Both are sanctioned by the Washington State Criminal Justice Training Commission. A 16-hour formalized training course is offered to those with time constraints.

Covered in Grady's course is a plethora of necessary topics such as dismounting the biked, riding stairs, and shooting. Some officers get a rude awakening when they are directed to ride six blocks at full speed, perform a tactical dismount and shoot accurately. The firearms portion of Grady's course, which uses 60 rounds, is held at the Seattle Police Department range and involves a quarter mile ride prior to shooting to simulate field conditions up to and including the donning of bicycle gloves while firing.

Grady's course breaks down as follows:
Nutrition (two hours)
Muscle Training (two hours)
Bicycle Injuries (two hours)
Bicycle Fitting (one hour)
Mountain Bike Nomenclature (two hours)
Mountain Bike Repairs (four hours)
Traffic Protocol (two to three hours)
Off-Road Riding (two hours)
Police Technical Skills (four to six hours)

Self Defense (two hours)
Firearms Training (two hours)
Course Evaluation and Practical/Written Test (two hours)

James O'Keefe, director of training for the New York City Police Department, echoed the topics and importance of training. "We teach the officers nomenclature, maintenance and repairs, nutrition, bike tactics and riding in traffic."

O'Keefe, a Houston police officer for ten years with a Ph.D. in criminal justice, oversees a staff at the Police Academy of 681 people including some 600 sworn personnel. An obvious proponent of training, he proudly pointed out, "We've trained over 950 uniformed officers."

His three-day course, modified from an earlier five day version, is taught at Floyd Bennett field and is recognized by the New York State Bureau of Municipal Police. The Las Vegas Metropolitan Police Department also conducts its training in-house. Schofield, a nine year veteran, said her agency mandates that all aspiring bikers qualify through a 40-hour (four day) school.

"We go over shifting, braking, mounting, tactical dismounts, technique riding, riding through crowds, patrol tactics, car and pedestrian stops, riding downstairs, and riding in traffic," she said. The southern Nevada agency has some 60 full-time and 12 part-time bikers prowling the streets and byways of Las Vegas.

But most agencies, which do not have their own in-house training apparatus, take part instead in area regional training. In the Central New Jersey municipality of South Brunswick Township, Community Policing Bureau Sergeant Pat Owens said they sent their four bike officers (who pedal part-time on a seasonal basis) to training at the nearby Rutgers University campus.

The Law Enforcement Bike Association has been instrumental in spreading not just the bike concept, but also the proper training regime which proves police biking is more than just a balancing act.

In Canada, five hours to the North of Billings, MT, the City of Calgary Police Department's Sgt. DeVillenfagne proudly pointed out that their regionally offered training is now sanctioned by the Law Enforcement Bike Association, as are a growing number of U.S. and international programs. Once a year, they offer a 40-hour course sponsored by the Calgary Police Department which is open to other agencies in the West. Grady said that regional bike training has been given a leg up by his bike association's six-day instructor school, which is held all over the country. The next instructor certification course is slated for Las Vegas, NV.

Equipment

Even given Calgary's harsh weather, many of their duties and training are the same as they ride the downtown business area year round. "We've added a turtleneck sweater for bad weather and deflate our tires to 30 pounds of pressure," explained Sgt. DeVillenfagne, supervisor of the eight constable bike patrol unit. The unit has braved temperatures of 30 degrees below zero (Fahrenheit).

Their Canadian fashion includes water-proof and wind-resistant foul weather jacket and pants. Their nylon duty belt has all the usual police accouterments with the addition of a cellular phone (reports are phoned in).

At the opposite end of the thermometer, Las Vegas has become known (thanks in part to extensive exposure of the TV show "COPS") for their trademark high-visibility yellow polo shirts. Added to the customized uniform mix is a light-weight jacket, a heavier jacket for winter, black nylon bike shorts and an expandable PR-24 baton.

Seattle's outfit is, as expected well-thought-out. In addition to a uniform shirt with cloth badge, the two-wheeled enforcers wear nylon bike shorts in the summer, helmet, and nylon web gear replete with .40 caliber Glock and ASP expandable baton. Cold weather brings out the turtleneck sweater and jacket with zip on sleeves. The cold weather gear is made from Ultrex (similar to Gortex) and is paired with gloves.

Central to the equipment picture is, of course, the bike itself. Seldom is the same care put into choosing a bike as is into selecting a patrol car. "You wouldn't go to the impound lot for a police car, because an officer depends on it, so you shouldn't go to the property room for a bike," Grady said. More is involved with bikes and a police bike should be replaced every three years (two years active and then one year on reserve status).

Seattle uses Raleigh FT 500 Police Special Editions, while Las Vegas Metro mounts up on Raleigh F300, F500, and MBOO bikes which sport a rear rack with bag for paperwork and flashlight. The agency puts 24 full-time bikers out on the famed Las Vegas strip has a retired bike officer who works 20 hours per week as a mechanic on the bicycles. New York's finest use Fuji American Police Model 21 bikes.

The purchase of inexpensive bikes compromises officer safety and (as Grady pointed out in his information packed book, "Policing by Mountain Bike") is not the route to take. Solid bikes ride in the range of $400 to $600.

It was emphasized by those interviewed that bikes should be assigned to individual officers and that the concept of fleet bikes be eschewed. Grady said that "Everybody shifts, brakes and rides differently," and assigned bikes make the equipment last longer. Schofield said that Las Vegas also assigns the bikes to the officer.

Funding for such an endeavor is available. In addition to grants covering the community oriented manifesto of the bike bet, some agencies have successfully applied drug forfeiture funds to bikes. Patrollers of housing authority areas have latched onto HUD funding.

The Seattle Police Department paid for the first seven months of their operation via a $500 donation from the Cascade Bicycle Club. The Tacoma, WA, Police Department received a grant from their downtown business association. Las Vegas' yellow-shirted riders came into existence via the largesse of the Las Vegas strip hotel owners.

"Among the other misconceptions out there is the choosing of a bike officer," said Grady, who said that they just don't look for experienced bike people. "We recruit officers that have tactical skills, are proactive, self-supervising and have public relations skills." Las Vegas looks for similar talents and only experienced patrol officers can see their transfer approved.

Seattle utilizes a $500 medical exam to assess the aspiring bike officer's suitability for a role which sees a riding routine of 15 miles a day (3,000 miles per year or the equivalent of riding from Seattle to New Jersey). The five-hour examinations includes a health history questionnaire, heart and lung examination, stress test, flexibility assessment, blood test to evaluate cholesterol and triglyceride, blood sugar and blood cell count, Cybex test on both knees and Hydrostatic weighing and spirometry.

A closer look at police bike patrols is warranted. The thoughtful implementation of such an endeavor yields a balanced approach to crime fighting and community relations that a department can ride into the next century.

September 1997
Law and Order:
The Magazine for Police Management

Academies Put Civilians in the Shotgun Seat: Law enforcement takes community policing to the next level

"The call goes out there's an armed robbery at the Whiskey River Bar and you are the patrol officer dispatched. At the scene you are confronted by a man running out of the door with a gun in his hand. You have to decide now: SHOOT or DON'T SHOOT."

That is the situation thrust over 1,000 citizens in the Central Florida area since the first Orlando Police Department's Citizens' Police Academy (CPA) was launched in 1985.

To bridge the gap between civilian and cop, law enforcement agencies are using CPAs to foster greater community interactions with the most misunderstood of professions- policing. Billed by some as the next level of community policing, CPAs are essentially mini-academies which allow a window into the local constabulary's service to the neighborhood.

In Orlando, community leaders, business executives, media representatives and other interested parties have had to make the above crucial decision whether to fire or not as part of a course held for 13 consecutive weeks. CPA participants are ushered into an empty police department auditorium, hold an unloaded department issued handgun at the ready, to confront a video scenario projected onto a screen.

"The tension is real and they get an understanding of the responsibility and the kinds of decisions officers have to make," explained Ilona Edwards, the Orlando officer who started the department's CPA.

"I held the same gun the officers hold, stopped cars they stop, and got a sense of what it is like stopping that car at 3:00 am that was weaving and had several people in it," said Steven V. Boyd, 44, a graduate of the New Castle County Police Department's 10th Citizens' Police Academy in New Castle, DE." Even though I was play-acting, my heart was thumping. It was kind of scary and I kept thinking I want to go home tonight."

Citizens' Police Academies cover topics from the officer's point of view including laws of arrest, search, and seizure, patrol operations, use of force, criminal investigation, S.W.A.T. operations, and traffic and DUI stops. This is all done in a civilianized, mini-police academy format conveniently scheduled in the evenings. Among the hands on components that make the classroom theory real are trips to the shooting range and to fire departments, as well as to the jail and an actual ride-along with a patrol officer on duty.

Franklin Township, NJ, Police Department Captain Joseph Linskey is a solid proponent of the Citizens' Police Academy idea. The suburban agency, located 40 miles from New York City, has already held one CPA with 18 participants and plans are in the works for more sessions.

Dencil C. Haycox, director of the Rio Rancho Department of Public Safety, a 90-square mile jurisdiction rubbing against the northwest border of the city of Albuquerque, NM, said that the three Citizens' Police Academies that they have held so far (each with 25 attendees) have helped raise the awareness of the 50,000 population jurisdiction. "This gives people an insight into what we do and where their tax dollars go," Haycox said.

"We're actively involved in community policing and this is the next step. It opens up what you're doing to the community," Linskey said. "The citizens involved essentially become ambassadors for our cause to the community and offer positive support for what we do."

Linskey said attendees of the first Franklin Township Citizens' Police Academy enjoyed the endeavor so much that those who missed one or two classes are clamoring to make up the lost sessions in the next CPA.

Boyd, an African American who works as a counselor for the Delaware Division of Human Relations said that the New Castle County CPA experience gave him a perspective from the other side of the badge that he can explain to his friends and co-workers, as well as to young people. "Rodney King was an unfortunate incident. I've been afforded a different point of view which fosters an atmosphere of understanding of why officers do what they do," Boyd said.

"I have known police officers, but never really understood what they go through on daily basis," echoed Peg Stewart, 38, another New Castle County CPA alum who works as a sign language interpreter and has a four-year-old son. "It was a little unsettling to fire a handgun, and I'm amazed people stay in the profession. So few people have a clue as to what officers go through."

Sandy Sanders, a 63-year-old small business owner who went through the Orlando program 18 months ago, proudly hangs his Citizens' Police Academy completion certificate on the wall. Sanders said he was impressed "with the caliber and quality of people on the force." He said he now defends Orlando officers when he hears people condemn them with no background investigation or familiarization with their job.

New Castle County's newly minted graduate Peg Stewart said she wished more people would attend the academy- particularly the media. "Recently, there was a bunch of letters in the newspaper downing the police for shooting a homeless man. But the letter writers and the media don't understand what officers face- we're not faced with that on a regular basis.

Orlando's Sanders said his experience has given him a new insight into law enforcement. "The newspapers are quick to jump on our officers without giving them credit. That's why I have become a civilian who acts as a spokesman speaking up on behalf of the officers."

New Castle County's high energy force behind their successful CPA, Corporal Verne Orndorff, said they particularly look for community leaders and people active in their neighborhoods to go through the program. They have developed a long waiting list of eager citizens.

The department has gotten favorable media exposure from reporters who have taken the CPA. The nearby Philadelphia-based ABC-TV station did a lengthy piece on it and the Wilmington News-Journal daily newspaper did a 15-part story on reporter Edward L. Kenney's participatory experience in what he dubbed "a crash course for law abiding citizens."

Orlando's Officer Edwards proudly pointed out that graduates of their CPA have formed an alumni association which is active in helping the officers of the

Central Florida agency in tangible ways as well. Every Christmas and Thanksgiving, CPA alumni come together and serve turkey dinners and breakfasts for 180 officers, as well as jail and communications staff, that have to work the holidays. A Winn Dixie executive, who also graduated from the CPA, arranged for the supermarket chain to donate the turkeys.

The Orlando Police Department's unofficial ambassador, Sandy Sanders, who serves as president of the Orlando CPA Alumni Association, said his group even arranged a personal thank you letter to each officer in the food line from area school children.

In another instance, a local Orlando hospital executive (yet another CPA disciple) has facilitated a catered setup every other month for eight years in the medical facility's cafeteria for departmental promotion ceremonies. Sanders said that their alumni association has a newsletter which updates their members on the department's activities and how the graduates can help with projects.

Mindful that not all might want to attend the Citizens' Police Academy for altruistic reasons, most agencies contacted have mechanisms in place to screen aspiring attendees. Additionally, all officers are careful as to what information is disclosed.

Corporal Orndorff and Captain Linskey indicated that they run "a cursory computer background check" on individuals. But Rio Rancho's Sergeant Griffith, who oversees their CPA, said they don't do any computer checks. He said they are extremely careful of the nature of the material discussed at the CPAs which are held at Intel Corporation's large Rio Rancho manufacturing facility.

"We don't go into specialized information and we don't compromise anyone's safety or the integrity of investigations," Griffith stressed. He also explained that their version also involves Emergency Response Team and video scenario firearms training simulations (F.A.T.S.) like the others.

New Castle County's questionnaire, a tool used by many for pre-screening, helped winnow their 100 applicants down to a manageable group of 32. Those selected reflected the department's quest for diversity.

Costs of a Citizens' Police Academy are minimal-particularly when weighed when weighed against the support, both tangible and intangible, that is garnered from the many influential people from the community who attend. "This is very inexpensive, and we get a positive effect," Linskey said. "We spent maybe $200 to print the manuals and provide coffee. The next time we expect that even those items will be donated. The time is also minimal as once the lesson plans are developed for the initial academy, there's not much additional work for future ones.

Rio Rancho's CPA is held in conjunction with three fellow New Mexico law enforcement entities (the

Sandoval County Sheriff's Department, the Corrales Police Department, and the Bernalillo Police Department) under a jointly funded community policing initiative.

All of the law enforcement officials contacted expressed a genuine interest in sharing their information with other departments. Orndorff said he has sent information packets to over 100 inquiring agencies in the United States, as well as others in Canada, France, and South Korea.

"This program makes the citizens a part of the police and the police a part of the community." Orndorff said. "This program is not to give these people a gun and a badge and turn them into cops. The aim is to have them take back what they learned to the community and foster a greater understanding.

April 6, 2010
PoliceLink.com

10 Tips for Ride-Alongs

Popular among law enforcers, aspiring officers, spouses of officers, dispatchers, community activists, journalists, and scholars, ride-alongs with on-duty police officers and deputy sheriffs have long been a fun-filled way to get a view from the other side of a particular department's windshield. Whether you are exploring the idea of a career in law enforcement, wanting a closer look at your local constabulary, or seeking that quality time with your fellow law enforcer or significant other, ride-alongs can be a positive learning experience that strengthens bonds, but can also be fraught with pitfalls.

Not all law enforcement agencies have ride-along programs. Those that do, view it as a powerful bridge to the community. Those that don't usually believe the liability issues in having civilians present in dangerous situations are too high. Some agencies do permit the practice, but may restrict it to certain types of folks. Examples of the people that may be allowed to participate include dispatchers, police officer job applicants, enrolled police academy cadets, criminal justice college students, college interns, or spouses of officers.

While riding along with a law enforcement agency can be fun, make no mistake about it. Ride-alongs are a dangerous activity. There have been instances of ride-alongs being present when officers are attacked and they witness other harsh realities of policing in America. This is not the sanitized TV version of COPS.

By the way, sworn officers sometimes participate in ride-along programs. They may want to ride with a friend in another agency in order to bond further or they may be interested in learning different police practices and operations. It is important that officers follow their department's and the host agency's policies as far as carrying weaponry and taking action to assist the on-duty officer. There are jurisdictional differences in laws and protocols that greatly affect how the guest officer conducts him or herself on the ride-along.

Suggestions geared to civilian ride-alongs obviously don't apply to sworn law enforcement personnel riding off-duty with other agencies or divisions within their department. Whatever the case, make sure you know your boundaries from the agency and the individual officer before you step into the car.

Having managed ride-along programs, had ride-alongs with me as a full-timer, and ridden along with officers in other agencies in the United States and overseas, I have picked up a few tips to help make your ride-along a more productive and enjoyable experience.

1) Do Paperwork. Ride-alongs in almost every agency I have ever seen involve the filling out of at least some paperwork. That paperwork usually encompasses a liability waiver that needs to be signed. Some agencies do allow minors to ride-along and those add a signature line for a parent or guardian. You may also have to read, agree to, and sign a departmental policy or booklet on ride-along rules. Other paperwork includes information and permission to run name, driver's license operator number, social security number, and date of birth information through law enforcement databases. Make sure that all of the information provided is true and correct. This paperwork facilitates conducting of an at least cursory background check. Law enforcement folks certainly don't want convicted or wanted criminals riding next to their officers.

2) Clear Up Warrants. And speaking of background checks, make sure that any warrants you may have are cleared up prior to applying for a ride-along. The police are not fond of wanted criminals riding with them, so they do check.

You laugh at the thought that someone would do this with an active warrant in the system, but I recall one young man that had requested permission to do a ride-along. Well, you can guess that his background check came up with a warrant for failure to appear (for court). I called him up and told him to come to the building, as his ride-along was ready. So, being a service-minded public servant, he got his ride-along as he wished-except it was in the back seat, not in the front seat. And it was only to the county jail. He even got a close up feel for handcuffs.

3) Wear Appropriate Clothing in Layers. As a ride-along in a marked police car, many folks will assume that you are some kind of detective or otherwise affiliated with the agency. You want to dress professionally, but still geared for a dynamic environment. I suggest business casual with comfortable shoes in the off chance you need to run out of the area. No shorts or jeans with holes or T-shirts (especially with questionable graphics or wording on it). Do not wear clothing articles with law enforcement logos or graphics. A collared polo shirt or button down shirt with khaki pants is appropriate.

Because officers wear bullet resistant vests, they tend to run hot, so they crank up the air-conditioning. As a result the front of the car can get quite cold. The use of layered clothing allows you to regulate your comfort without infringing on the officer. There can also be quite a temperature difference from being inside the car to being outside the vehicle. The use of layered clothing enables you to manage that issue as well.

4) Don't Touch Radios, Computer, etc. Most officers will give you a tour of the car when you start the shift. Very importantly, they'll show you the radio that is their lifeline to communications. As the officers and telecommunicators in PoliceLink-land know, the dispatcher is an important person to the responding law enforcer. If they are in trouble, the radio is the conduit for getting help.

Don't play with the radio or change the frequency channel. Officers are very protective of the controls in their "cockpit." If they do instruct you to call for help, or you have to do so when they can't, press the button on the side of the microphone for a moment to allow the repeater to kick in. Then talk clearly and succinctly. Let go of the button to allow the dispatcher and other units to talk. Be sure to know which is the radio microphone and which is the public address (P.A.) mike.

And while we're at it, don't touch the radio to change the station or CD. Depending on departmental regulations, some officers with take home cars are able to install satellite radio, CDs, and other audio devices. The same goes for the in-car computer. This is their mobile office and they spend eight, ten, twelve plus hour shifts in this environment. They have preferences on how things are arranged and will not appreciate a visitor altering things without being requested to do so.

5) Eating Etiquette. Officers work hard and rely on each other in sometimes life-threatening situations.

Eating on meal breaks is an important part of the culture of policing. Sitting at the table literally will give you an understanding of their world and their perspective.

Let the officers pick the eatery. You should eat prior to going on duty since you may have a high call volume shift and be unable to stop. If you and your host officer are able to take a break, the picked establishment may not be the type of food you would normally eat. Pick food off the menu wisely, so that you don't end up needing the officer to make a high speed run to a bathroom.

While many agencies have policies that prevent officers from accepting free or discounted food, it is not your place to discuss it at that point in public. If a discount is not extended to you as a civilian guest, you certainly should not pound your fist and demand that your bill be adjusted. On the contrary, if you are able to, I suggest you pick up the tab for the officers present in appreciation for them including you in their world. If the restaurant management insists on cutting the bill, you should leave a tip on the table that equals or exceeds the full-price check.

6) Less Talk, More Listen. Many folks when engaged in their first ride-along get quite excited. That leads to the motor mouth syndrome. Officers tend to be reserved when they first meet their ride-along. They are unsure of the person's motivations or perspective at first. It is better to go slow and allow the officer to get to know you. In an adaptation of the old adage, it is better to be

quiet and listen than to speak and be thought of as a fool. It should without saying that profanity and other unprofessional speech has no place. These guidelines are particularly true of you are an aspiring officer applying to the agency as they are checking you out as much as you are learning about them.

7) Confidentiality. Law enforcement officers see quite a bit of interesting stuff in their line of work. Even Hollywood can't make up what officers see in real-life. As a participant in a ride-along, you may see neighbors and other people from your community at their worst moment. Specifics and identifiers from the call are not for public consumption unless otherwise agreed upon. Some agencies may allow you to attend the pre-shift briefings. Again, information being discussed is not public in nature and you need to use discretion in discussing what you have seen and heard.

Notable exceptions pertain to the presence of credentialed media and news journalists who are approved for the ride-along with the full knowledge of their objective. Famous examples include the TV show "COPS."

On the local level, having a news crew onboard is a win-win situation. The department gets to showcase officers engaged in good policing and reach out to the community via the viewing audience. The TV station gets some great visuals that draw people to their newscasts especially during crucial ratings sweeps periods (that set advertiser rates).

As a police chief, I approved local network affiliates' news cameras to ride-along with patrol personnel in marked Ford Crown Victorias. We thoroughly discussed the rules and boundaries beforehand and each time it proved to be a rewarding experience for all concerned. These are folks who will reveal information publicly and have been approved to do so in advance by the nature of their mission.

8) Shotgun Release. Much like the radio, the officer may show you how to use the shotgun release in case events break bad and help from you is needed. Don't be like a certain ride-along that kept playing with the shotgun release during a call. Pushing the button and moving the shotgun repeatedly will make for a very nervous officer. It's best to trip the release only when you and the officer really need you to do so.

9) No Weapons, Handcuffs. Unless you are a sworn officer from another agency who is allowed to have your police firearm and equipment with you, don't bring a gun, handcuffs, or the like on the ride-along. Most agencies have rules that prohibit such items even if you have a carry concealed weapon permit or license (CCW).

The only exception to the police equipment guidance offered is to wear a bullet resistant or ballistic vest. As a patrol division deputy sheriff, I had a spare vest in the trunk of my marked Chevrolet Caprice that I had ride-alongs wear. If you have your own, you may want to wear it hidden under your outer shirt.

10) Follow Instructions. The most important of the ten tips in this PoliceLink column is to follow the instructions of both the department and the host officer or deputy sheriff. This is a major liability and responsibility for the agency and the officer.

Be aware that not all officers may be happy with your presence. Some police officers view their world as being closed to non-sworn folks, while others will welcome you with open arms. The law enforcer may or may not like ride-alongs.

Whether the officer volunteered or was volunteered by their supervisors certainly makes a difference in the quality of the ride-along experience. Even more crucial though is whether you listen to what you are supposed to do. Following instructions will go a long way towards creating good will.

For example, many agencies require that the ride-along stay in the car during calls for police service. If that is the case, do so unless the officer has you move for safety or other reasons.

Ask questions to clarify your limitations and instructions before you begin the adventure. If you fully understand your boundaries and follow instructions, your ride-along experience will be a terrific two-way bridge of understanding for you as a member of the community and for the law enforcer serving the community.

Appendix

Partial Listing of Published Articles by
Dr. Richard Weinblatt

Examiner.com June 30, 2010
"Policing the Twilight, Drake and Justin Bieber beats"

Examiner.com June 30, 2010
"Why police should suspect missing Kyron Horman's stemom"

Examiner.com June 27, 2010
"Police shift tactics at G20 Global Economic Summit in Toronto"

Examiner.com June 27, 2010
"Reality TV show cop Betsy Brantner Smith: women police have come far"

Examiner.com June 27, 2010
"Detroit Police: proud of crime stat. murder rate drop"

Examiner.com June 24, 2010
"Experts question Joran van der Sloot's police blame game"

PoliceLink.com June 11, 2010
"You're In Trouble: Now What?"

PoliceOne.com June 5, 2010
"Police to Professor: Making the Move to Academia"

PoliceLink.com May 28, 2010
"10 Ways to Generate Complaints on Patrol"

PoliceLink.com April 22, 2010
"10 Rules for Police Resumes"

PoliceLink.com April 6, 2010
"10 Tips for Ride-Alongs"

PoliceLink.com March 11, 2010
"10 Tricks for Picking the Right Department"
Newark Advocate (OH) & NewarkAdvocate.com
January 15, 2010
"Police Academy Students Pursuing their Dreams"

PoliceLink.com October 15, 2009
"The Bottom Line of Seat Belts for Law Enforcers"

PoliceLink.com October 1, 2009
"10 Domestic Violence Reminders for Veteran
Officers"

PoliceLink.com September 2009
"Ten Tips for On Target Academy Firearms Training"

PoliceOne.com August 25, 2009
Weinblatt's Tips column: "Top 10 social networking
tips for cops"

PoliceOne.com August 3, 2009
Weinblatt's Tip column: "There's a New Sheriff in this Media Town"

CNN AC360 Anderson Cooper blog (guest writer on Anderson Cooper's CNN.com blog) - July 30, 2009 "Gates, Crowley and The President: Calling it how I see it"

PoliceLink.com July 24, 2009
"Response to National Racial Debate: Gates, Crowley and the President"

PoliceLink.com January 2009
"Bad Credit, Bad Applicant"
Domestic Preparedness Journal September 10, 2008
"When Disaster Strikes: Gaining Peace of Mind"

PoliceLink.com August 25, 2008
"Professionalism: What Does Your Badge Stand For?"

PoliceOne.com August 22, 2008
Weinblatt's Tips column: "P1 Exclusive: What law enforcement can learn from the Caylee Anthony case"

PoliceLink.com August 2008
"Answering Common Oral Hiring Board Questions"

PoliceLink.com July 2008
"10 Tips for Mastering the Police Oral Board"

PoliceOne.com May 16, 2008
"National Police Week: Reflecting on our
vulnerabilities"

PoliceLink.com April 2008
"Getting Serious About Joining the Force"

PoliceLink.com November 26, 2007
"Ten Tips for Dealing with the Opposite Sex"

PoliceLink.com November 20, 2007
"Surviving Your Prisoner Transport"

PoliceOne.com November 16, 2007
Weinblatt's Tips column: "10 Taser tips for LEOs"

PoliceLink.com October 30, 2007
"Promotions: The Courses That Count"

PoliceLink.com July 2, 2007
"So you wanna be a cop… First impressions count!"

PoliceOne.com April 20, 2007
Weinblatt's Tips column: "Tips for major incident
media relations in the wake of the Virginia Tech
shooting"

PoliceOne.com February 16, 2007
Weinblatt's Tips column: "10 tips for officers engaged
in off-duty incidents"

PoliceOne.com March 6, 2006
Weinblatt's Tips column: "PoliceOne Exclusive:
Domestic disturbance response: 10 tips for winning at
these volatile calls"

Officer.com March 6, 2006
Reserve Power column: "The Flip Side: Why Some
Reserves Hate Cops"

Officer.com February 17, 2006
Career Corner column: "How to Keep Your Boss
Happy: How to acquire power in the agency"

Officer.com February 6, 2006
Reserve Power column: "Why Some Cops Hate
Reserves: A crack in the police family"

PoliceOne.com January 16, 2006
The Police and the Press column: "Press releases: Used
and abused"

Officer.com January 16, 2006
Career Corner column: "Inside the FBI National
Academy: The FBI NA and Others are Key to
Promotion"

PoliceOne.com January 4, 2006
Weinblatt's Tips column: "Police officer suicide
prevention: Officers kill themselves at higher rate than
general population"

PoliceOne.com January 3, 2006
Weinblatt's Tips column: "PoliceOne members respond"

Officer.com January 3, 2006
Reserve Power column: "The Ultimate Sacrifice: Line of Duty Deaths Underscore Officers' Service"

Officer.com December 16, 2005
Career Corner column: "Academic Jobs for the Cop: How to Land those Teaching Gigs"

PoliceOne.com December 14, 2005
Weinblatt's Tips column: "Creative cuffing for small-wristed subjects"

Officer.com November 22, 2005
Reserve Power column: "The Original Homeland Security Force: For volunteer cops, it's the same old 'thang'"

PoliceOne.com November 21, 2005
Weinblatt's Tips column: "10 tips for talking with kids"

PoliceOne.com November 10, 2005
Weinblatt's Tips column: "Searching for a clue"

PoliceOne.com November 10, 2005
Weinblatt's Tip column: "Death notifications: A tough police assignment"

PoliceOne.com November 10, 2005
Weinblatt's Tips column: "Carrying a knife: Officer safety and administrative considerations"

PoliceOne.com November 10, 2005
Weinblatt's Tips column: "10 ways to minimize complaints"

PoliceOne.com November 10, 2005
Weinblatt's Tip column: "Firearms training: train like you play"

PoliceOne.com November 10, 2005
Weinblatt's Tips column: "Crime scenes: stopping the evidence eradication gremlins"

PoliceOne.com October 26, 2005
Tip: "Returning DL can help avoid consent problems"

The Orlando Sentinel (daily newspaper Orlando, Florida) October 19, 2005
Editorial: "A rip in fabric that holds law enforcement together"

PoliceOne.com October 19, 2005
The Police and the Press column: "The absence of a police marketing mentality"

Officer.com October 19, 2005
Career Corner column: "The Good, the Bad, and the Ugly of Online College Degrees"

PoliceOne.com October 12, 2005
Officer Safety Tip: "Officer safety: It's not just an on-duty thing"

PoliceOne.com October 3, 2005
Training Tip: "AlcoSensor breath samples: How to tell if your subject is cooperating"

PoliceOne.com September 26, 2005
Officer Safety Tip: "The forgotten piece of equipment: handcuffs"

PoliceOne.com September 19, 2005
Officer Safety Tip & Training Tip: "Intersection safety for backup units"

PoliceOne.com August 30, 2005
The Police and the Press column: "Putting a human face on the police: Making an emotional connection"

PoliceOne.com May 24, 2005
The Police and the Press column: "P1 Exclusive: Ten Tips for Working with the Media"

PoliceOne.com April 4, 2005
The Police and the Press column: "How History Makes the Future of Police Media Relations Clearer"

PoliceOne.com April 28, 2004
The Police and the Press column: "The Image in the Mirror: The Enemy has a Face"

The Courier-Tribune (daily newspaper Asheboro, North Carolina) Friday, April 23, 2004 Guest Column: "Appreciation for a job well done"

American Police Beat April 2004
"How to give yourself a good shot at the job: Don't shoot yourself in the foot before you even get to the interview"

The Courier-Tribune (daily newspaper Asheboro, North Carolina) Sunday, January 4, 2004
Guest Column: "Understanding your partnership with your police"

Sheriff Magazine January-February 2003
"Sheriffs' Psychologists: The Ultimate Backup for the Progressive Sheriff's Office"

Law and Order: The Magazine for Police Management May 2001
"Alaska's Reserves Brave the Elements"

Law and Order: The Magazine for Police Management May 2000
"Departmental Gyms Become Fitness Rooms: Final Phase in a Holistic Fitness Approach"

Law and Order: The Magazine for Police Management May 2000
"Beyond Hurricanes: Riots, Bombings are 21st Century Reserve Duties"

Law and Order: The Magazine for Police Management
April 2000
"Solving High Tech Crimes: Private and Public Sector Partnerships"

Corrections Technology Management Magazine
March/April 2000
"Role-Playing"

Law and Order: The Magazine for Police Management
February 2000
"Creative Funding Makes AEDs a Reality in Patrol Cars"

Law and Order: The Magazine for Police Management
January 2000
"Volunteers Assist in Private/Public Sector Partnership

Law and Order: The Magazine for Police Management
December 1999
"The Paramilitary vs. Academic Training Debate"

Law and Order: The Magazine for Police Management
December 1999
"Managing Off-Duty Jobs: A Clear Policy Is The Key To Success"

Corrections Technology and Management Magazine
November/December 1999
"So You Want To Be a Volunteer Probation Officer"

Law and Order: The Magazine for Police Management
November 1999
"Bridging Gaps in Assignments: Villa Park Fills in with
Auxiliary and Part-time Officers"

Law and Order: The Magazine for Police Management
October 1999
"IACP Conference 1999: Charlotte: The Queen City"

Law and Order: The Magazine for Police Management
October 1999
"Charlotte-Mecklenburg Police: 21st Century
Technology and Community Service"

Law and Order: The Magazine for Police Management
October 1999
"The Shifting Landscape of Chief Jobs: What's Changed
and How to Forge a Path"

Law and Order: The Magazine for Police Management
September 1999
"Agencies Look to Year 2000: Assess Y2K Options"

Law and Order: The Magazine for Police Management
September 1999
"Volunteer SPCA Officers: Working with Local Police
to Protect Animals"

Law and Order: The Magazine for Police Management
August 1999 "Special Report: New Training Concept:
New Police Training Philosophy: Adult Learning Model
on Verge of Nationwide Rollout"

Law and Order: The Magazine for Police Management
August 1999 "RCMP Takes Learning to the Streets"

Law and Order: The Magazine for Police Management
August 1999
"The Evolution of Police Footwear: It is the Era of Air
Jordans and Bloodborne Pathogens"

Law and Order: The Magazine for Police Management
May 1999
"Discovering a Valuable Asset: Reserve Search and
Rescue Units"

Corrections Technology Management Magazine
October 1998
"Come Fly With Me: Feds Take to the Air to Help
Locals with Safe, Economical Inmate Moves"

Corrections Technology Management Magazine
May/June 1998
"Point-Counterpoint: Weighing in on Privatization"

Law and Order: The Magazine for Police Management
May 1998
"Changing the Corporate Culture: How One State
Agency Took on the Challenge"

Corrections Technology Management Magazine March
1998
"Locals Get A Piece of the Action from Uncle Sam:
Strapped Jails Turn Finances Around: Facilities Garner
Federal Prisoners and Dollars"

Law and Order: The Magazine for Police Management
February 1998
"Reserve Expertise Makes Air Support A Reality"

Corrections Technology Management Magazine
February 1998
"Point-Counterpoint: Showdown in the Arizona Desert:
Maricopa County's Tent City Jail"

Law and Order: The Magazine for Police Management
December 1997
"Negative Perceptions Common: Regulars Question
Value of Reserves"

Police: The Law Enforcement Magazine October 1997
So You Wanna' Be a Police Chief: Aspiring to the Top
Rank of Law Enforcement Today Takes More
Experience, Training, Education, Skills, and Political
Savvy Than Ever Before"

Law and Order: The Magazine for Police Management
September 1997
"Academies Put Civilians in the Shotgun Seat: Law
Enforcement Takes Community Policing to the Next
Level"

American Police Beat June 1997
"Is The Grass Greener at the Aurora, Colorado Police
Department?"

Law and Order: The Magazine for Law Enforcement
Management June 1997
"Riding with Reserve FTOs: Field Training Programs
Vary in Different Departments for Reserve Officer
Recruits"

Sheriff Magazine March-April 1997
"Sheriffs Take on Rural Patrol Challenge"

Law and Order: The Magazine for Police Management
April 1997
"Special Report: Bicycles: More Than Just a Balancing
Act"

Law and Order: The Magazine for Police Management
April 1997
"Rank Insignia for Reserves: Debate Revolves Around
Public Perception and Officer Acceptance"

American Police Beat March 1997
"The Paychecks are High and So Is Morale"

Law and Order: The Magazine for Police Management
March 1997
"Special Report: S.W.A.T.: Counseling and Support for
S.W.A.T. Personnel"

Sheriff Magazine January-February 1997
"Sheriffs Find Innovative Solutions: Providing Jail
Medical Services with Limited Funds"

Law and Order: The Magazine for Police Management
December 1996
"Advice for Reserves: The Reserves' Legal Eagles and
Insurance Icons Weigh In"

Police: The Law Officer's Magazine October 1996
"Have Gun, Will Travel: Gaining Certification in the
New Frontier"

Law and Order: The Magazine for Police Management
September 1996
"Reserve Duties Vary in the Bay State: Massachusetts
Officers Wear Many Hats"

Law and Order: The Magazine for Police Management
April 1996
"Reserve Officers Man Boats: Turnover is Low for
Police on the 'Baywatch' Beat"

Law and Order: The Magazine for Police Management
March 1996
"Reserves Patrol on Bicycles: This New Breed is
Cutting a Wide Path as they Pedal Forth"

Law and Order: The Magazine for Police Management
November 1995
"Take-Home Cars for Reserves: Officer Effectiveness
and Community Presence Enhanced by Program"

Law and Order: The Magazine for Police Management
August 1995
"A Class Act: University Police Reserves Pass the Test of Professionalism"

Law and Order: The Magazine for Police Management
April 1995
"N. Carolina Reserves Among Top Ranked: Volunteers Find the Sweat and Hard Work are Worth It"

Law and Order: The Magazine for Police Management
February 1995
"P.E.P. Program: Part-Time Officer Training in Illinois"

Law and Order: The Magazine for Police Management
December 1994
"Liaison Officers: A Vital Link in a Reserve Operation"

Law and Order: The Magazine for Police Management
September 1994
"Oral Boards Go High-Tech"

Law and Order: The Magazine for Police Management
August 1994
"Police Footwear Meets the 'Reebok Generation'"

Law and Order: The Magazine for Police Management
August 1994
"Battle Dress Utility"

Law and Order: The Magazine for Police Management
June 1994
"Seasonal Reserves: Part-time Paid Personnel Fill in the Gaps"

Law and Order: The Magazine for Police Management
April 1994
"Reserves, Regulars and Regulators: How They Work Together in New Mexico"

The Narc Officer March/April 1994
"Reserve Heroes"

Law and Order: The Magazine for Police Management
February 1994
"Reserves Mount Up: Provide Services Otherwise Curtailed"

Law and Order: The Magazine for Police Management
December 1993
"Professionalism Reduces Liability: Trained Reserves Make Positive Contribution"

Law and Order: The Magazine for Police Management
October 1993
"Reserves Excel in the Sunshine State: Training Exceeds Standards"

Law and Order: The Magazine for Police Management
August 1993
"Reserve Data Available: New Book Provides Everything You'll Want to Know"

Police: The Law Officer's Magazine July 1993
"Credence & Credibility: Training, Selection Standards, and Liability Still Top The List of Concerns About Reserve Officers. Increased Professionalism, However, Has Brought Increased Respect"

Law and Order: The Magazine for Police Management June 1993
"Reserve Motorcycles: A Positive Public Relations Impact"

21st Century Policing Summer 1993
"Volunteer Officers and Community Policing"

Law and Order: The Magazine for Police Management April 1993
"Reserve Detectives"

The F.O.P. Journal Spring/Summer 1993
"Reserve Policing: Stepping Stone to a Career"

Law and Order: The Magazine for Police Management February 1993
"'Freelance' Reserves"

Law and Order: The Magazine for Police Management December 1992
"Reserve Wildlife Officers: A Different Breed"

Law and Order: The Magazine for Police Management October 1992
"Reserve K-9"

Law and Order: The Magazine for Police Management
August 1992
"The Thin Line Between Reserve and Full Time"

Law and Order: The Magazine for Police Management
April 1992
"Alabama Reserves Alive and Well"

Law and Order: The Magazine for Police Management
February 1992
"The Police and The Media"

Law and Order: The Magazine for Police Management
February 1992
"The Golden State of California Reserves"

Law and Order: The Magazine for Police Management
December 1991
"The Birth of a Volunteer Officer Program"

The Police Investigator October 1991
"Hostage Incidents: The Experts Respond"

Law and Order: The Magazine for Police Management
October 1991
"The State of the State Reserve Trooper"

Law and Order: The Magazine for Police Management
September 1991
"Accreditation: A Force Affecting Reserve Officers"

The TMPA Quarterly July 1991
"Texas Reserve Cops: The Lone Star State is Pioneering the Way"

The Narc Officer February 1991
"The Use of Reserve Officers in the War on Drugs"

The Reserve Law Officer 4th Quarter 1990
"Does TV Depict 'Real Life' Police Work?"

www.ingramcontent.com/pod-product-compliance
Lightning Source LLC
Chambersburg PA
CBHW050130280326
41933CB00010B/1318